Models

Helen and Peter McNiven

With photographs by Chris Fairclough

Thomson Learning • New York

FIRST ARTS & CRAFTS

Books in this series

Collage
Drawing
Making Masks
Models
Painting
Printing
Puppets
Toys and Games

For Harry

First published in the
United States in 1995 by
Thomson Learning
115 Fifth Avenue
New York, NY 10003

First published in Great Britain in 1994 by Wayland (Publishers) Ltd.

Library of Congress Cataloging-in-Publication Data
McNiven, Helen.
  Models/Helen and Peter McNiven; with photographs by Chris Fairclough.
       p.   cm.—(First arts & crafts)
First published in 1994 by Wayland (Publishers) Ltd.
Includes bibliographical references and index.
ISBN 1-56847-214-5
  1. Models and modelmaking—Juvenile literature. 2. Paper
work—Juvenile literature. [1. Models and modelmaking.
2. Paper work.] I. McNiven, Peter (Peter Alister). II. Fairclough,
Chris, ill. III. Title. IV. Series.
TT154.M23   1995
745.592'8—dc20   94-22442

Printed in Italy

Contents

A small world   4

A sculpture from a drawing   6

An artist's room   8

Vegetable market   10

Wild West town   12

Animals from natural forms   14

Bobbing driftwood boat   16

A beach scene at home   18

Grow your own   20

Minimonster mobile   22

Junk skeleton   24

Totem pole   26

The big E   28

Helpful hints   30

Glossary   31

Index   32

A small world

From the earliest times people have made small copies of the world around them, to amuse themselves and their children. We still make models today. Modern toys and models are often made of plastic, but they are just as much fun to make from things we can find.

The Queen Mary's dollhouse, The Museum of Childhood, Bethnal Green, England.

Perhaps the best thing about models is that we can make our own little world and imagine ourselves in it when we play with them.

In this book you will discover how to make exciting, colorful models from everyday materials. You will find out how to look out for things in nature (called natural forms) that can be made into something very different.

Always be on the lookout for materials with colors, textures (how things feel), and patterns that you can use to make your models.

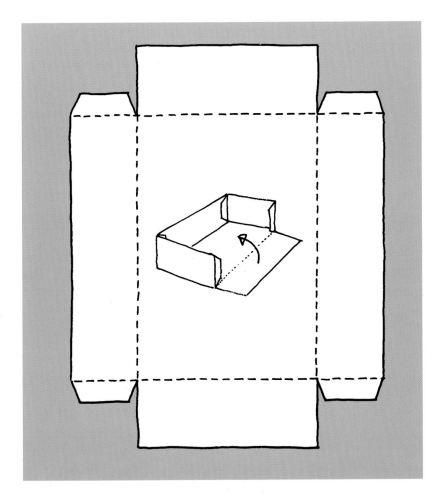

A box is the first thing you'll need for many of the projects. You can do a lot with this simple object. It can be cut, stuck, flattened, added to, folded, and disguised. You can use cardboard boxes that you find at home. You can use the diagram here to make your own boxes from paper, cardboard, and other materials.

A sculpture from a drawing

When we draw, we are putting lines on a flat surface – a drawing of someone or something is flat. But most things are not flat. Look at your face and then feel it. It has bumps and hollows and there is space around it.

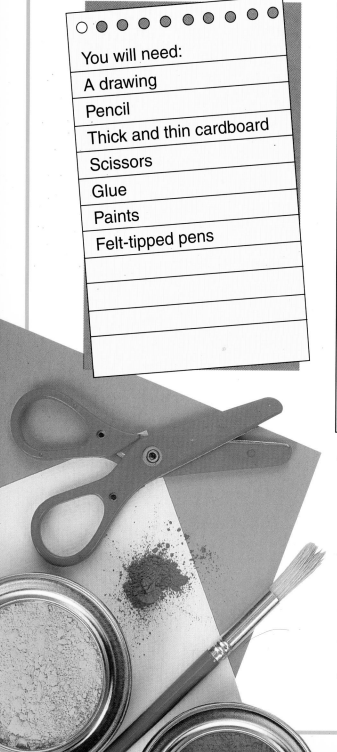

You will need:

A drawing

Pencil

Thick and thin cardboard

Scissors

Glue

Paints

Felt-tipped pens

Synthetic Construction (Black and White) (1965-66) by Victor Pasmore (born 1908).

Sculptures have space around them. Artists think about how to show space using colors and shapes. Look at this construction by Victor Pasmore. It has different shapes and levels. It plays with space. You can do this too.

- Make a drawing of anything you want.
- Copy or trace one part of your drawing onto a piece of cardboard. Copy another piece on to some thicker cardboard.
- Cut them both out. Some of the drawing's background can be cut out and used as a shape, too.
- Color the pieces brightly on both sides.
- Glue the pieces of your drawing onto a cardboard base. Display your new model where other people can enjoy it.

An artist's room

You can make a famous painting into a model. Look at this calm but colorful picture of a bedroom by Vincent van Gogh.

You will need:

A cardboard box

Cardboard

Scissors

Glue

Paints

Felt-tipped pens

Bedroom at Arles by Vincent van Gogh (1853-1890).

The painting is flat, but we can see a floor, walls, and furniture in different parts of the room. The artist has shown us how this room looked.

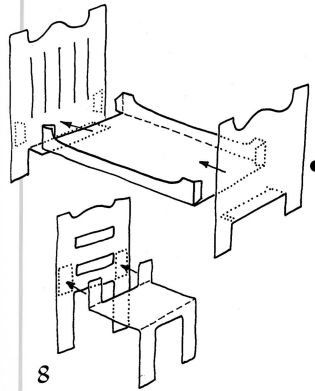

● Find a cardboard box — a shoe box is ideal. Cut it so that you have a base (floor) and two sides (the walls). Don't worry if your sizes are not the same as those in the picture.

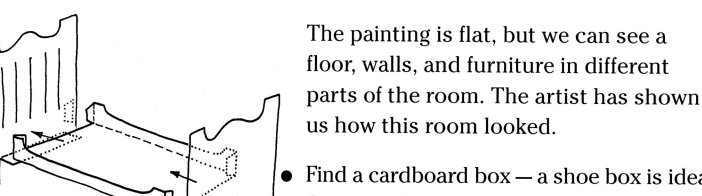

- Cut a door and windows out of the walls, or paint them on. Or glue on pieces of cardboard for the door and windows.
- Cut out or fold pieces of cardboard to make other things in the room. Try to include everything.
- Paint your room brightly, like the picture, or choose your own colors.
- Look for other paintings of rooms. You could make a model of your own room.

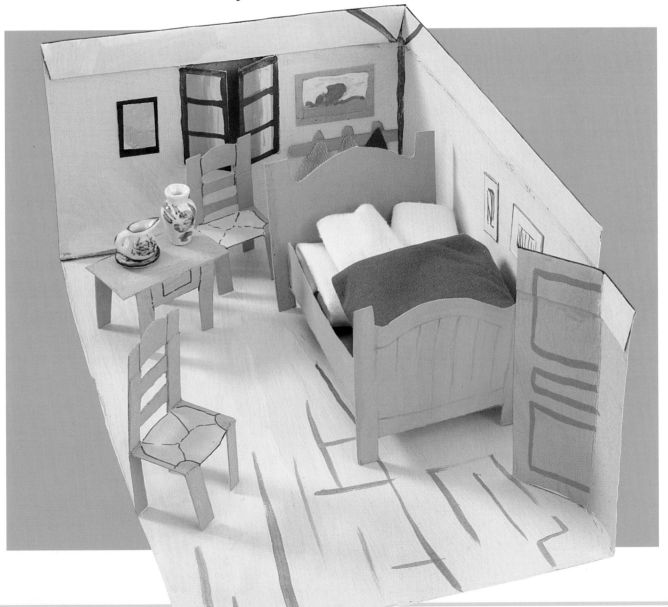

Vegetable market

Here is a painting of a flower shop by Richard Estes. The artist stood outside the shop and painted it. Next time you go to the store, look at it from the outside.

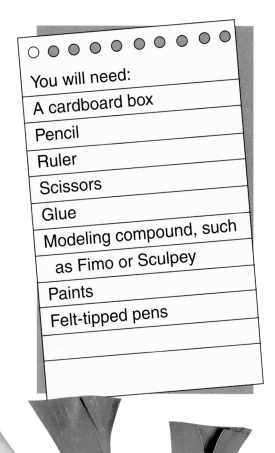

You will need:

A cardboard box

Pencil

Ruler

Scissors

Glue

Modeling compound, such as Fimo or Sculpey

Paints

Felt-tipped pens

Flower Shop (1969) by Richard Estes (born 1936).

Look at all the things you can buy in stores and at how they are laid out. Look at colors, shapes, and sizes of the things for sale.

You can make a vegetable market from a cardboard box and then make all the things to go in it.

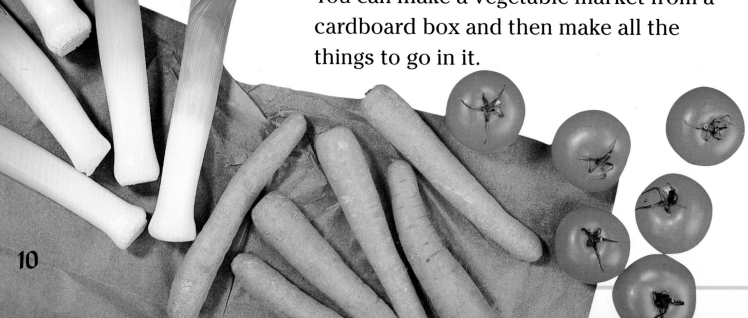

- Mark a big cardboard box as shown. Fold in one flap for a canopy.
- Cut out from A to B, from B to D and from A to C. Fold along lines C to D and E to F. Now you have a window and a counter.
- Cut from G to H, from G to I, and from I to J. Now you have a door. Cut a window in the door.
- With modeling compound, make all the things you want to sell in your market.

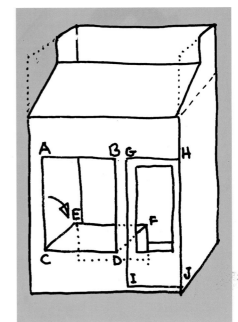

- Paint your finished model. As you paint, think about colors you've seen in shops and how those shops were painted.

Animals from natural forms

Animal Head (1956) by Henry Moore (1898 -1986).

You will need:

A collection of natural
 forms
String
Glue
Paints
Buttons and beads
Colored paper

So far you have used manufactured forms to make your models. Now you can try using natural forms.

Artists have always made use of the things around them. Look at this sculpture by Henry Moore. It might remind you of rocks or driftwood.

- Collect leaves, sticks, bark, or pebbles that make you think of other things — especially animals.
- Make sure all your finds are clean and dry.
- Join them together with glue or string, or balance them on top of one another.
- Add eyes, a nose, and a mouth with paints, or glue on things you find around the house, like buttons, beads, or colored paper.
- See how many different animal sculptures you can make.

Bobbing driftwood boat

Look at pictures of boats. Look at their shapes and colors. Sometimes they have sails or flags.

You will need:

Driftwood

Toothpicks

Paper

Paints

Thread

Cardboard

Ruler

Scissors

2 matchboxes

Glue

Wooden skewer

Modeling compound

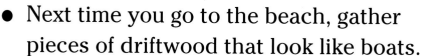

- Next time you go to the beach, gather pieces of driftwood that look like boats.
- When you have a piece you like, make small holes in the top and push in toothpicks for masts.
- Make sails and flags out of paper and color them brightly. Glue them onto a piece of thread and tie them to your masts.

To make your boat bob, cut out a piece of cardboard that measures 8 inches by 9 ½ inches. Paint on a sky. Cut out your sea from more cardboard, measuring about 8 inches by 3 inches.

- Glue a matchbox to both sides of the sky background near the bottom. Glue the sea background on top, as in the diagram.

- Make a hole through the sea, the boat, and the sky. Push a toothpick through them all (see picture). Make a hole in the bottom of the boat. Push in a wooden skewer with a fish made out of modeling compound on the other end. Your boat will seem to bob on the water when you give the fish a push.

A beach scene at home

Everybody loves the shore with its colors, sounds, and smells. You can have a beach at home all the year round. Here is a beach scene painted by one of the authors of this book.

You will need:

Paints and paper

A shallow cardboard box

Fabric and cardboard

Sand and pebbles

Small boxes

Cocktail umbrellas

Egg cartons

Toothpicks

Scissors

Modeling compound

Matchsticks

The Beach at Quatre Vaux by Peter McNiven (born 1952).

Look at all the different things in the picture: the sea, the sand, rocks, people, trees, umbrellas, tents, and flags. Look at all the shapes and colors.

- Draw or paint a beach scene.
- To make a model of your scene you need a shallow cardboard box. You can paint on sea, sky, and sand, or use blue fabric for the sea and real sand.

- Add all the things you have seen. Make brightly colored beach huts from small boxes and make flags and umbrellas from cocktail umbrellas and toothpicks. Make rocks from egg cartons painted brown and green or add real pebbles.
- Cut out people, or make them from modeling compound. You could make a pier with toothpicks and cardboard.
- Make towels, windbreaks, and deck chairs from paper, fabric, and matchsticks. Pack your scene full of the fun of the seaside.

Grow your own

This model can really help things grow. The trapped heat of the sun and warm, damp air make seeds grow shoots much more quickly. People often put seeds in a special house called a greenhouse. Here is a picture of a very famous British greenhouse.

The Palm House at Kew Gardens, London, England.

You will need:

2 clear plastic containers

Scissors or knife

Clear tape or glue

Popsicle sticks or
  construction paper

Matchboxes

Small pots

Egg cartons

Plastic bottle caps

Seeds

Compost

- To make your own greenhouse, cut one plastic container as shown. Ask an adult to help you.
- Cut out the bottom of the other container, leaving a half-inch rim all the way around. Glue or tape the containers together.
- Decorate the containers with strips of construction paper or Popsicle sticks, glued on to look like wood. You can make shelves inside with Popsicle sticks and matchboxes.

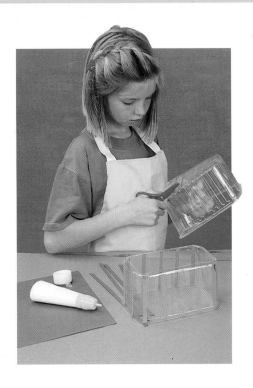

Your greenhouse is ready. Fill small pots, egg cartons, or plastic bottle caps with compost. Plant seeds, like sunflower or pumpkin seeds.

Minimonster mobile

You will need:

Corks

Paints and felt-tipped pens

Gardening wire

Pencil and ruler

Glue

Tissue paper

Scissors

A pin

Small beads

Garden sticks

Thread or fishing line

There are insects all around us. Some are so small we cannot see them; others only come out at night. Lots are brightly colored.

Look at this mobile by American sculptor Alexander Calder. The brightly colored hanging shapes balance and move in the air.

You can make a mobile of butterflies and dragonflies.

Blue Boomerang (1958) by Alexander Calder (1898-1976).

For the body: Paint corks one color or striped and leave them to dry.

Wings: Cut a 6-inch length of garden wire, make a loop, and twist the ends together. Do this three more times. Put glue around the wire and stick on tissue paper. When the glue is dry, trim around the loops. Decorate the tissue paper with felt-tipped pens. Make holes in each side of the cork with a pin and glue on the wings.

Legs: Use other pieces of wire to twist around the middle of the cork. Make into four or six legs. Thread and twist beads onto the ends.

Antennae: Wrap a 2-foot piece of wire around the cork and twist the two ends toward the front. Take each antenna and lightly wrap it around a pencil, like a spring. Then remove the pencil and thread on some beads.

Make a cross with garden sticks. Hang insects from each end and in the middle with thread.

Junk skeleton

Now let's think bigger! Models don't have to be small; they can be huge. With this project you might want to work with friends, and you will need adult help. This project is easy to make with everyday materials and some imagination.

You will need:

An assortment of household packagings

String or wire

Coat hangers

Newspaper

Pencil

Scissors

Knife

Mexican Day of the Dead celebration, California.

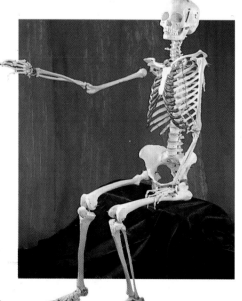

Inside your body you have bones. All these bones together are called your skeleton. Without a skeleton you would not be able to move. You can have great fun making a skeleton from things found around the home. Try to make the skeleton join together and bend the way you do.

First, lie down on a big piece of newspaper or several pieces of newspaper taped together and ask someone to trace you. Mark all the places where you can move, such as shoulders and knees.

Gather together all sorts of things for the skull and bones—the funnier, the better. Lay them out on your plan and join them together with string or thin wire.

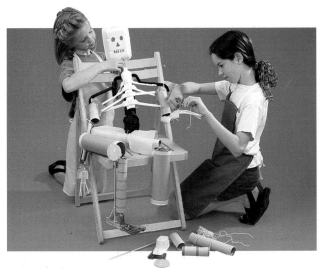

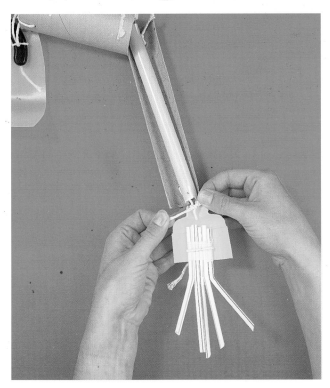

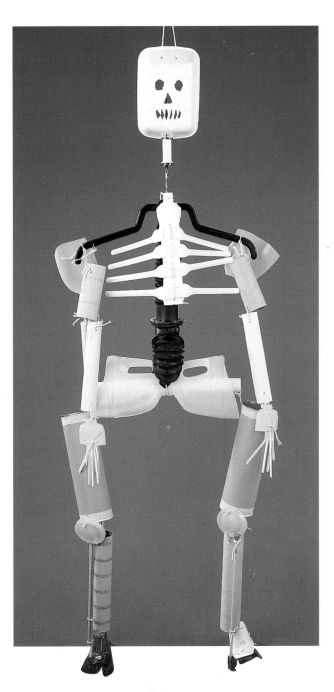

Totem pole

For many centuries Native Americans carved wooden models of the animals they saw around them. They used the trunks of huge pine trees. Sometimes they decorated them with beads, feathers, shells, bones, string, and leather.

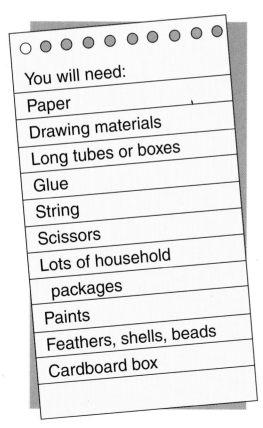

You will need:

Paper
Drawing materials
Long tubes or boxes
Glue
String
Scissors
Lots of household packages
Paints
Feathers, shells, beads
Cardboard box

Totem pole in Queen Elizabeth Park, Victoria, Canada.

We call these carvings totem poles. You can make your own totem. It can be as big as you like.

- Look at lots of animals and birds in pictures or, if you can, go to a zoo. Look at their markings, fur, feathers, paws, and claws. Look at their ears, eyes, and noses.
- Now make a drawing of the animals' heads, one on top of another.
- Make a central pole of tubes (you can get long poles from fabric or carpet stores).
- Glue or tie shapes and boxes in the shape of animals, one on top of another, to the central pole. When you have stuck on your basic shapes, paint them brightly.
- Add feathers, shells, and beads to make your totem look really magical.
- Glue the bottom tube into a large cardboard box to make a secure base.

The Big E

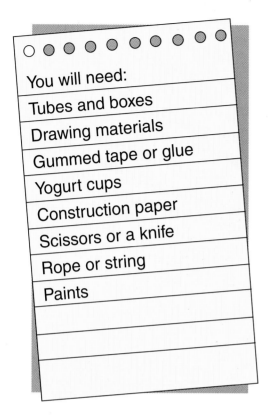

You will need:

Tubes and boxes

Drawing materials

Gummed tape or glue

Yogurt cups

Construction paper

Scissors or a knife

Rope or string

Paints

Of all the amazing creatures in the world the elephant must be one of the strangest. Artists have drawn them. Kings have kept them as pets. Warriors have used them in battle. They are used in India to work and to carry important people.

You can make your own elephant with some friends. Look at this photograph of an elephant and see how big its legs, body, head, and trunk are. Gather together boxes, tubes, and cartons – make sure they are big.

- Make four towers the same height out of boxes. These will form the legs. Now attach them to four large boxes glued together to make a body. Does the body slope? Is it the same width all the way around? Look at elephant pictures and walk around your sculpture —now you are really thinking like a sculptor.
- Build a head at one end. Try to shape the box like a real elephant's head —wide at the top and pointed toward the trunk.
- Use tubes or yogurt cups for a trunk, or roll up some construction paper. Do the same for tusks. Add on big flapping ears made from construction paper and a rope tail.
- Paint your elephant with gray paint, or pink if you must!

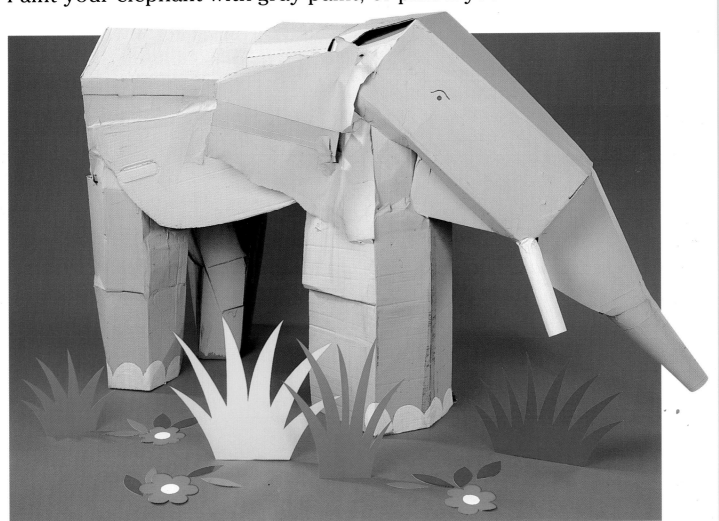

Helpful hints

You can make models of just about anything, from train stations to African plains. You don't need expensive materials, just a great imagination and an eye for what *could* be. A foam tray from a package of fresh fruit could be cut up to make people or animals. A magazine picture of a blazing fire could be cut out and framed with Popsicle sticks to make a dollhouse living room elegant! Keep your mind open and your eyes peeled and you'll be able to use ordinary things to make extraordinary models!

Here are some helpful hints:

- Keep all of your model ideas in a notebook. When you are looking through old magazines, tear out pictures that give you ideas and glue them into your notebook.

- Get big cardboard boxes at stores, where they sometimes give away their empties. Save small cardboard boxes, such as shoe and jewelry boxes. Save the sheets of cardboard that dry cleaners and shirt manufacturers fold into shirts.

- Keep buttons, beads, foreign coins, pretty stamps, and other items that might come in handy for decorating a model. Store them in one of the boxes you are saving.

- Draw your model on a flat surface so you can decide if the finished product will be pleasing *before* you do lots of work.

- Make models of things that you have seen, but also make models of things in your imagination, such as a haunted castle, a house on another planet, or a monster from the middle of the earth.

- Spread newspaper before you work. Clean up after yourself.

- Ask a friend to make models with you.

Glossary

Antennae The two feelers on the head of an insect. They are used to touch and smell things.

Centuries A century is 100 years.

Disguised Made to look like something else.

Driftwood Wood floating on or washed up by the sea.

Manufactured Made by people.

Mobile A sculpture that hangs in the air.

Native Americans The very first people to live in America.

Patterns Shapes and colors that are repeated.

Sculptor A person who makes sculptures.

Sculptures Models or figures made out of solid materials.

Shutters Wooden doors covering windows, which can be closed to shut out the sun.

Veranda A porch on the outside of a building, where people can sit.

Further information

Further Reading

Craig, Diana. *Making Models: 3-D Creations from Paper and Clay.* A First Guide. Brookfield, CT: Millbrook Press, 1993.

Making Models and Games. Crafts in Action. North Bellmore, NY: Marshall Cavendish Corp., 1993.

Maxwell, Colin. *Model Making.* Fresh Start. New York: Franklin Watts, 1992.

O'Reilly, Susie. *Modeling.* Arts & Crafts. New York: Thomson Learning, 1993.

Index

animals 14-15, 26-27
    elephant 28-29
beach 16, 18-19
boat 16-17
drawing 6, 7
greenhouse 20-21
minimonsters 22-23
mobile 22-23
Native Americans 26

nature 5, 14-15
sculptures 6, 15, 22, 29
seaside 16-17, 18-19
seeds 21
shop 10-11, 12
skeleton 24-25
street 12-13
totem pole 26-27

Acknowledgments

The publishers wish to thank the following for the use of photographs:
The Queen Mary's dollhouse p.4 by courtesy of the Board of Trustees of the Victoria and Albert Museum.
The Tate Gallery, London for *Synthetic Construction (Black and White)* 1965-66 p.6 by Victor Pasmore.
Visual Arts Library for *Bedroom at Arles* p.8 by Vincent van Gogh and *Flower Shop* 1969 p.10 by Richard Estes © DACS 1994.
Popperfoto for Main Street, Creede, Colorado p12.
Animal Head 1956, bronze edition of 10 by Henry Moore p.14 © The Henry Moore Foundation.
Christies Images for *Blue Boomerang* (mobile) p.22 by Alexander Calder © DACS 1994.
Mexican Day of the Dead celebrations, San Juan Bautista, California p.24 ©Andy Jillings.
All other photographs © Chris Fairclough Colour Library.

The publishers also wish to thank our models Kim, Kerry, Manlai, Katie, and Jeremy, and our young artists Harry, Sophie, and Jack.